FIFTY
FASHION
LOOKS
THAT
CHANGED
THE
1950s

**DESIGN
MUSEUM**

FIFTY
FASHION
LOOKS
THAT
CHANGED
THE
1950s

**PAULA
REED**

THE
1950s

British rockabilly style in action in 1957. The skirt of this gingham dress would have been held out with layers of net petticoat.

1951 evening dresses by Cristóbal Balenciaga, inspired by the paintings of Henri de Toulouse-Lautrec. *Below* A Christian Dior dress from 1955.

THE
1950s

The 1950s marked a sea change in fashion. And nothing would ever be the same again. Change came faster than hits in the pop charts. Fashion was emerging from behind the closed doors of the gilded salons, the exclusive preserve of the rich and titled, and was bursting onto the street. Customers of all ages and from all social backgrounds lapped up the new, sybaritic energy after years of wartime deprivation.

A younger generation, finding its voice for the first time, began to use clothes to express themselves, exploring fashion's power as a symbol of identity: a mark of belonging and of difference. Defining the generation gap was becoming big business for the marketing men, and fashion was one of their most effective tools.

Fashion pages, for generations the preserve of the fashion magazine, were in demand from a much wider audience. Popular newspapers were no longer complete without a fashion desk, a fashion editor and a regular fashion headline, and as a result, trends became the dynamic engine driving sales. New easy-care fabrics and systems of mass production coupled with comparative prosperity enabled Mrs Average, everywhere, to be the best-dressed woman in the world.

A model lounging on a bed, wearing Claire McCardell's pink-and-white striped dress of 1952. *Below* Christian Dior's black taffeta dinner ensemble of 1951. Rounded hip and shoulder lines, tiny waist and high bustline are achieved with a short, fitted jacket atop a voluminous skirt.

THE DUKE AND DUCHESS OF WINDSOR

High style

History does not look fondly on the Duke (1894–1972) and Duchess (1896–1986) of Windsor, one of the most controversial couples of the twentieth century. Their affair started while she was still married to her second husband, Ernest Simpson. In spite of being heir to the British throne, Edward's *raison d'être* became simply to be married to Wallis Simpson.

The world was stunned by the news that the American commoner had somehow seduced the man who was now king. Many wondered aloud: What could he possibly see in her? Give up the throne for – what? Sex? Wallis is credited with icily stating, 'No man is allowed to touch me below the Mason–Dixon Line.' There were also ugly and persistent rumours questioning her physical female endowments. And then there were the stories of her affairs, Nazi sympathies and shopping.

Nonetheless, the couple were fêted in fashionable society as the ultimate trendsetters. Wallis Simpson was known for her impeccable manner of dress, her extensive and precious jewellery collection, and her taste in interior design. He, as the Prince of Wales and later the Duke of Windsor, was also known as the 'Master of Style'. Men's fashion reverberates with his influence to this day. He is still widely referenced as one of the best-dressed men in all of history, with a personal style that was flawless, at times quirky, and always legendary. 'Did he have style?' Diana Vreeland once asked rhetorically. 'The Duke of Windsor had style in every buckle on his kilt, every check of his country suits.'

The Duke and Duchess's shared interest in fashion offers a glimpse into the reasons for the longevity of their relationship. Wallis Simpson once remarked: 'My husband gave up everything for me. I'm not a beautiful woman. I'm nothing to look at, so the only thing I can do is dress better than anyone else. If everyone looks at me when I enter a room, my husband can feel proud of me. That's my chief responsibility.' Her approach to her marriage was always to make the Duke feel like he was still the King.

In terms of style, hers was more restrained than his. He was an emblem of elegant hedonism. She liked simple, tailored clothes, without unnecessary detail or decoration. The photographer Cecil Beaton once said, 'She reminds one of the neatest, newest luggage and is as compact as a Vuitton travelling case.'

GYPSY ROSE LEE
'Let me make you smile'

'Let me entertain you,
Let me make you smile…' The influence of Rose Louise Hovick (1911–70), whose 1957 memoir, *Gypsy*, became a Broadway smash and a film starring Natalie Wood, resonates still through the style and stage presence of burlesque stars such as Dita Von Teese. Bought up in the grinding poverty of the 1940s, the former child performer propelled herself from rags to riches through a combination of wisecracking repartee and business brains, as well as beauty. At an evening at the New York Public Library to celebrate the centenary of her birth, Karen Abbott, author of a biography of Rose, said: 'If Lady Gaga and Dorothy Parker had a secret love child, it would have been Gypsy Rose Lee.'

Born in Seattle in 1911, Rose worked in vaudeville alongside her sister, June, but while June had the makings of a star, Rose had no discernible talent at all. She only discovered by accident that she could make money in burlesque when a shoulder strap on one of her gowns gave way, causing it to fall to her feet. The audience applauded her desperate efforts to cover herself, and so she decided to make the 'accident' the focus of her performance.

She became one of the biggest stars of Minsky's Burlesque in New York, where the huge audiences were as likely to include longshoremen as the city's intelligentsia. Her style was a send-up of a striptease act, with the emphasis firmly on the 'tease'. She brought a wry sense of humour to her act which, in a world singularly lacking in sophistication, propelled her to mainstream stardom.

She got big laughs as she dropped the pins that held her costumes together into the tuba in the orchestra, and fussily straightened the crooked black bow on her nipple with an 'Oh dear!' She revealed little actual flesh, ending the act draped coyly by the curtain. The act was really more about comedy than sex, and men *and* their wives were often in the audience.

Gypsy Rose Lee's wardrobe of feather boas, ostrich fans, corsets and lace may well owe something to her mother's first career as a seamstress and milliner. Mrs Hovick specialized in extravagant hats and exotic lingerie, and spent months on the road visiting mining towns and lumber camps from Nevada to the Yukon, selling the flashy apparel to prostitutes.

HARDY AMIES
Understated English elegance

'A woman's day clothes must look equally good at Salisbury Station as the Ritz bar,' said Sir Hardy Amies, summing up his understated British style. He made his professional home on Savile Row, the home of British bespoke tailoring, and specialized, as he himself said, in a quiet English elegance that 'didn't frighten the horses'.

Born in 1909 in Maida Vale, West London, Amies grew up to become one of the most important postwar names of British fashion. His mother, a *vendeuse* in a smart ladies' outfitters, introduced him to London couturier Lachasse for his first job in 1934. During World War II he served in British Intelligence.

Amies opened his own house on Savile Row after the war in 1945, financed by the Countess of Jersey, the first Mrs Cary Grant. To most, he will always be remembered for dressing the Queen. The association began in 1950, when Amies made several outfits for the then Princess Elizabeth's royal tour to Canada. And, although the couture side of the Hardy Amies business was traditionally less financially successful than the menswear business, the award of a Royal Warrant as official dressmaker in 1955 gave his house international kudos.

Highlights in his career also included a triumphant if unlikely collaboration with Stanley Kubrick, for whom he created costumes for the futuristic epic *2001: A Space Odyssey* (1968). He was also something of a commercial alchemist, managing to grow his business until it was worth more than £200 million.

Paris may have been the home of the scene-stealing fashion heroes, but Hardy Amies was the quintessential English couturier of the age. As he himself once said, 'I can't help it. I'm immensely impressed by all genuine upper-class manifestations.'

Hardy Amies may have become famous as the Queen's official dressmaker, but he also made a significant contribution to fashion history as a menswear designer. In fact, thanks to his use of men's tailoring techniques in womenswear, he is often considered one of the first proponents of power dressing.

LISA FONSSAGRIVES-PENN

'A good clothes hanger'

The Swedish-born model Lisa Fonssagrives-Penn (1911–92) inspired some of the most famous photographers of the 1950s, working with Horst, George Hoyningen-Huene and Irving Penn. The Russian-American magazine editor Alexander Liberman has said of her: 'It is difficult to imagine the history of fashion photography without thinking of Lisa Fonssagrives-Penn.'

Born Lisa Bernstone, she had trained as a dancer but turned to modelling when work fell off. She was featured so frequently in the fashion pages of *Vogue* and *Harper's Bazaar* that her face, it was said, was as recognizable as the Mona Lisa. In 1948 she became the first model to make the cover of *Time* magazine. In the course of her career she hung perilously from the iron spars of the Eiffel Tower for Erwin Blumenfeld, disrobed for Horst and parachuted over the Paris skyline for Jean Moral.

In the late 1940s, when most models were paid $10 to $25 an hour, she was earning $40 an hour. When most models' careers ended before their thirtieth birthdays, hers flourished until she was past 40. She married Penn in 1950.

After her death in 1992, Liberman said, 'She was the inspiration and subject of some of Penn's greatest photographs. She epitomized a very noble period of fashion and couture. She gave a classical dignity to anything she wore.' Lisa Fonssagrives-Penn, however, had a more down-to-earth attitude to her contributions as a model. In the 1948 article in *Time* magazine, she was quoted as saying: 'It is always the dress, it is never, never the girl. I'm just a good clothes hanger.'

Fonssagrives' famous poise was down to her early ballet training. Asked how she maintained her figure, she always insisted on the importance of eating little and often, up to ten meals a day. But to her, a meal might mean only six grapes, a single slice of cheese, one cracker and half a glass of wine. 'Always eating, but never anything much' was her motto.

KATHARINE HEPBURN

Nonconformist style

A reluctant style icon, Katherine Hepburn (1907–2003) was the daughter of a suffragette who became the poster girl for androgynous chic. She appropriated a masculine style of dressing, but unlike Dietrich who had gone before her, she wore little make-up, preferring to be natural and comfortable rather than glamorous. As a child she desperately wanted to be a boy, cutting her hair and adopting an alter ego named 'Jimmy'.

She had been wearing trousers, which were then considered quite unladylike, since the 1930s. Her style of dress and her outspoken manner didn't always endear her to the Hollywood pooh-bahs, at a time when the blonde bombshell was the general idea of a silver-screen star. And yet, as one contemporary fashion magazine noted, 'she almost singlehandedly broke down the dress code for women' by insisting on wearing men's trousers both on and off the set.

In 1993 she declared, 'I realized long ago that skirts are hopeless. Any time I hear a man say he prefers a woman in a skirt, I say: "Try one. Try a skirt."' It is said that she never owned a dress or skirt of her own. She popularized the plain colour palette and the oversized silhouette that she loved. The elements of the Hepburn look – wide-legged pleated trousers, flat loafers, soft mannish shirt and easy tailored jacket are the instantly recognizable ingredients that constantly resurface on catwalks to this day. In 1986, the actress was recognized by the Council of Fashion Designers of America for her role as a nonconformist in twentieth-century fashion.

It was said that when the costume department removed her trousers from the dressing room, Hepburn refused to put anything else on and walked around the studio in her underwear until they were returned. She was one of the few great Hollywood stars who made no attempt to sugar-coat her personality, a personality that was blunt and feisty. Her abiding motto was: 'if you obey all the rules you miss all the fun.'

NORMAN NORELL
'Dean' of American couture

Norman David Levinson (1900–72), from Indiana, became
Norman Norell when he moved to New York to study fashion
illustration at Parsons School of Design. He started his working
life in the costume department of Paramount Pictures, before
meeting his mentor, Hattie Carnegie, in whose design studio he
worked for 12 years, learning to curb his dramatic tendencies.
Nevertheless, the rumour goes that he left over an argument with
Ms Carnegie about the suitability of a sequined skirt he had designed
for actress Gertrude Lawrence in *Lady in the Dark* (1944).

Setting out on his own, he was the first winner of the prestigious
Coty Award in 1943. After the war, American designers still
specialized in copying what happened on the Paris catwalk, but
Norell was one of the few to win the respect of Parisian couturiers.
In 1953 the New Yorker declared he 'was the fastest with lines that
will later show up with Paris labels'.

Throughout the 1950s, Norell honed his skill for combining
day and evening elements. He showed lavishly full-skirted
shirtwaist dresses in watered silk or lace combined with organdie.
He combined satin-collared tweed jackets with satin ball gowns.
He made trench coats out of taffeta and fitted white collars and cuffs
on daytime shirtwaisters as well as silk ball gowns. He was famous
for his sequined dresses that, with their slithery, skinny silhouettes,
became known as 'mermaid dresses'.

As the 'Dean of American Fashion', Norell was the first to have
his name on a dress label, and the first to produce a successful
American fragrance with a designer name.

In this deceptively simple
dress, the 'mushroom' pleats
hang in plumb-line straight
panels when the wearer
stands still, and billow out
when she moves. At the
time, the outfit was offered
at a retail price of $195.
When American fashion
trailed behind Paris and
London, Norell's simple but
stylish clothing was praised
for its glamour, classic
timelessness and the quality
of its construction.

NYLONS
Wartime's most wanted luxury

Throughout much of the 1940s the production of nylon stockings stopped, as nylon production was commandeered to help in the war effort. Production of parachutes and tents could not be interrupted for a fashion accessory, however morale-boosting. With the war over, the hosiery industry was allowed to gear up again and the demand for nylons rocketed. Demand was so great that sales quotas were imposed; riots broke out when promoters made special offers.

Nylons had been introduced to the market back in 1940, and not much had changed in the intervening decade. Without any qualities of stretch, they had to be 'fully fashioned' in a wide variety of sizes to fit all legs exactly. The seam down the back was not a fashion detail: it was created when the stockings were knitted together. However, at a time when nylon stockings were hard to come by, mimicking this seam with a steady hand and an eyebrow pencil could create a convincing impression of one of the war's most unattainable and coveted luxuries.

Freed from the exigencies of war, the hosiery technology of the 1950s progressed at a pace, and yarn manufacturers discovered they could add stretch by crimping nylon under heat. By 1959, DuPont was ready to launch Lycra, which could stretch to up to seven times its original length without breaking or changing shape. The days of the fully fashioned stocking were over, and circular knitting machines eliminated the need for seams.

When the war ended, Macy's entire stock of 50,000 pairs of nylons sold out in six hours. A newsreel from the time exclaimed, 'Nothing did more to brighten the postwar scene than the reconversion of the hosiery industry. A man with a pair of nylons in his pocket was better off than a GI in Germany with a hatful of chocolate bars.'

CHRISTIAN DIOR

The New Look

12 February 1947: a world that was slowly emerging from the deprivations of war was stunned by Christian Dior's couture collection. For women accustomed to improvising their wardrobes, the Dior 'Corolle' collection (named after the delicate petals at the centre of a flower) was an irresistible seduction. 'It's quite a revelation, dear Christian,' pronounced Carmel Snow, editor of the US fashion magazine *Harper's Bazaar*. 'Your dresses have such a new look.'

Key elements were sloping shoulders, narrow waists and full hips. 'I wanted my dresses to be constructed upon the curves of the feminine body whose sweep they would stylize,' said Mr Dior. In place of uniforms, he wooed women with traditional images pilfered from a romanticized past. Tiny waists were achieved with corsets called 'waspies'; the skirts were stuffed with petticoats. The world was midway through the twentieth century, but the New Look restored Paris to the pinnacle of high fashion with a wardrobe that owed much to the Victorians.

Women loved it. The couture house was inundated with orders. Dior was invited to London by the royal family, although King George V forbade the princesses Elizabeth and Margaret from wearing the New Look, lest it set a bad example at a time when rationing was still a reality for most.

But the trickle-down effect was immediate. From the Sears catalogues that took fashion to the remotest corners of the US to the poodle skirt and ponytail worn by teenagers everywhere, the Dior look defined postwar exuberance in fashion. The New Look did not, however, outlast Dior's death in 1957 – perhaps because the design was so impractical for the growing number of working women. However, the wardrobes of the 1950s were defined by Dior's creation.

Dior achieved tiny waists with a 'waspie' corset. Hips were padded, and definition was accentuated with peplums on jackets and bustles on skirts. He used push-up bras to fill out the bust line, and full skirts were stuffed with petticoats. There was so much interlining, boning, stiffening and corsetry that it was said a New Look dress could stand up all on its own.

JACQUES FATH & BETTINA
Le style parisien

In the history of 1950s fashion, Christian Dior's shining star tends to eclipse all others. But Jacques Fath (1912–54) was also a dominant influence on postwar fashion. His was a short-lived but meteoric career. He opened his house in 1937 and died of leukaemia in 1954. During that time, he also mentored the fledgling careers of Hubert de Givenchy and Valentino Garavani.

During World War II, Fath was known for 'wide fluttering skirts', which, the *New York Times* explained, 'he conceived for the benefit of women forced to ride bicycles during gasoline rationing'. His clients included Ava Gardner, Greta Garbo and Rita Hayworth, who wore a Fath dress for her wedding to Prince Aly Khan.

But he is best remembered for creating a look for the spirited, chic Parisienne, offering a younger alternative to the styles of Balmain and Dior. And it was the 'supermodel' Simone Micheline Bodin Graziani (1925–), pet-named 'Bettina', who defined her. With her red hair and fresh face, Bettina personified the modernity, wit and accessibility of Fath's brand.

Magazine fans of the time may not all have been able to afford a Fath original, but they slavishly copied the details – his bathing-cap hat, long evening gloves pushed down to the wrist for daywear, rhinestone earrings and bracelets, and a string of graduated pearls were the accessories of the moment. Bettina may have famously lent her name to an iconic blouse by Hubert de Givenchy from his first collection, but in interviews she has often cited her formative Fath years as the highlight of her career.

Fath's bold silhouettes, dramatic necklines and unorthodox flourishes – such as the 'flying saucer buttons' popularized by Bettina and Hollywood starlets – have reverberated down the generations, through the styles of Viktor & Rolf, John Galliano and Giambattista Valli.

In an interview, Bettina explained the chemistry: 'He liked that I was "different": I wore no make-up and I had red hair. At the time, he was interested in conveying an American spirit and a brand-new attitude. He wanted to communicate a modern image to the media. So I became the face of Fath.'

LAUREN BACALL
One of the boys

Lauren Bacall (1924–) was a beacon of no-nonsense practical style in an era of feminine excess. One of the boys, she was considered an honorary female member of the Rat Pack in the 1950s.

She started out as a model, getting her big break as an actress when she was discovered on the cover of *Harper's Bazaar* by the wife of director Howard Hawks, Nancy. It was Mrs Hawks who encouraged her to change her name from Betty Joan Perske to Lauren Bacall, had her voice trained to speak in a lower, more masculine tone, and suggested she tilt her trembling chin downwards in screen tests to hide her nerves.

Bacall's wardrobe was an extension of her acting style: utilitarian, razor sharp and fuss-free. She could carry off mannish tweeds and a trilby as well as any of the guys. Arguably, her style had more to do with the practical 1940s than the fragrant 50s. Her best accessories were her knowing look and glacial poise. She told *Vogue*: 'For my peculiar face I look best when I look as though I am not wearing any [make-up].' And when it came to clothes she told the magazine she preferred 'nothing itsy-bitsy – you shouldn't have to do too much to them, just wear them.'

In an era of the high maintenance wardrobe Lauren Bacall steered a course towards effortless minimalism. Statement jewellery and attention-grabbing accessories were not her thing. Her simple tailored clothes were a backdrop for what many fans tried but could not quite so easily copy – her steely allure and enigmatic femininity. Her iconic loosely waved coiffure never had a hair out of place, yet her faultless grooming seemed a foil for her feisty and unconventional nature.

In their day, Humphrey Bogart and Lauren Bacall (photographed here with their son Steve) were the ultimate 'It' couple. Although their relationship was at first controversial (she was 21, and he was married and 45), most agreed they were made for each other. When they were finally pronounced man and wife, the groom kissed the bride and the bride said, 'Oh, goody!'

RENÉ GRUAU
Exuberant flourish of line

In the late 1930s, when photography began to replace *Vogue*'s celebrated illustrated covers, the demand for fashion illustration went into dramatic decline. By the 1950s, René Gruau (1909–2004) stood alone as a star in a world that was increasingly dominated by photographers.

His style was instantly recognizable for its broad, sweeping brushstrokes. Using Indian ink and gouache, his drawings were an exuberant flourish of line on a background of flat colour. His stylistic influences ranged from the kabuki theatre and Japanese art, then at the height of fashion, to the lithographs of Toulouse-Lautrec.

Above all, however, Gruau is recognized for his visual wit and storytelling. It was these that enabled him to engage his audience in an innately sophisticated way reflecting not only his skill as an accomplished commercial artist but also his canny sense of marketing and advertising, at a time when those industries were still in their infancy. He worked for clients throughout the world of luxury and the arts. He was in demand as much as a designer of ballet sets and costumes as of film posters; he was as capable of depicting cars and brandy as well as haute couture.

But it was his fashion work that made him a superstar. He collaborated with many of the luminaries of the golden age of couture, including Balmain, Givenchy, Schiaparelli and Fath. It was his work with the House of Dior that gained him a reputation. Beginning with Dior's New Look in 1947, Gruau had a long relationship with the couture house that continued into the late 1990s. The 2011 Spring/Summer Haute Couture Collection of Christian Dior by John Galliano was heavily inspired by Gruau's works.

What set Gruau apart from (and often at odds with) his peers was that much of his best work was done for commercial purposes: advertising and marketing. But Gruau's work was an elegant and powerful stimulus at a time when the French fashion industry needed a boost to get back on its feet again.

CRISTÓBAL BALENCIAGA
Re-creating the silhouette

Born in Getaria, Spain, in 1895, Cristóbal Balenciaga carved a reputation early in his career as one of the few couturiers able to cut, fit and sew his own designs. Forced out of Madrid by the Spanish Civil War, in 1937 he opened his couture house in Paris on the fashionable avenue George V, where his peers were Chanel, Schiaparelli and Mainbocher.

He continued to work in Paris throughout World War II, although it was not until the postwar years that he truly shone. The 1950s were his decade. The silhouette he created was different from the hourglass shape of the New Look that had made Christian Dior the toast of Paris. Balenciaga favoured fluid lines and experimented constantly with the way fabrics related to a woman's body.

In the course of the decade, Balenciaga cut a swathe through classic silhouettes, reworking shoulder lines and raising and dropping waistlines regardless of natural shape. In 1953 he introduced the balloon jacket, enveloping the upper body in a cocoon that appeared to lengthen the legs and set the face on a kind of pedestal. The year 1955 saw the launch of the tunic dress, and in 1957 came the high-waisted baby doll. His cocoon coat and his balloon skirt, shown as a single pouf or doubled, one pouf on top of the other, were in huge demand.

Considering how the waist was the focal point of the classic 1950s silhouette, it speaks volumes about his influence that neither of his most popular designs – the sack dress of 1957 and his chemise dress of 1958 – had one. To this day Balenciaga remains influential, having achieved fashion's most elusive goal: the creation of a unique and totally new silhouette.

During the 1950s, it was said that a woman 'graduated' from Dior to Balenciaga. Dior was never jealous of Balenciaga's superior skills. Balenciaga was the man Dior called 'maître'. A long-time client offered a fitting epitaph: 'Women did not have to be perfect or even beautiful to wear his clothes. His clothes made them beautiful.'

BARBARA GOALEN

The first British supermodel

1953

It was in the 1950s that models first became household names. And Barbara Goalen (1921–2002) was arguably the first British supermodel – before the term was even invented. The best could earn handsome salaries: five guineas an hour, as much as the average weekly wage for girls in ordinary jobs. And because it looked so easy and glamorous, they inspired a generation of hopefuls who had no idea of the discipline that was involved.

In addition to being the consummate professional, Barbara Goalen also had the magic genetic ingredients that often define the extraordinary. Her 33-18-31-inch figure and her weight that never exceeded eight stone combined with an innate elegance to make her a perfect clothes-horse for the New Look. A widow with two small children, at 24 she became a couture model in a fashion showroom. Her big break came when she met the photographer John French, who at once recognized her photographic potential.

From 1950 Barbara Goalen appeared continually in *Vogue* and *Harper's Bazaar*; it was said she could make the simplest cotton dress look like the height of chic. She personified the aloof sophistication that was the code for elegance throughout the decade, and looked perfect in highly stylized clothes.

In the postwar years, models could achieve film star status. Designers started to talk about them as their inspiration or 'muses'. Barbara Goalen's clothes and doe-eyed makeup were widely copied, and her exploits were followed in gossip columns from the time she started working with photographer John French until her marriage to the Lloyd's underwriter Nigel Campbell in 1956. Crowds of fans mobbed the couple at Caxton Hall, Westminster, where the wedding took place.

After the wedding, and while still at the top of her profession, she retired from modelling and had two more children.

Goalen epitomized the priviledged English classes and refused to compromise her lofty standards. After her retirement as a model, her fashion column in the *Daily Telegraph*, in the liberated 1960s, insisted on elbow-length black gloves with a cocktail frock, and an above-elbow pair with a strapless ballgown: on the other hand, she happily played 'straight woman with arched eyebrow' opposite the Goons.

THE BIKINI

The most important thing
since the atomic bomb

The invention of the modern bikini is claimed by the French engineer Louis Réard in 1946. He is said to have named it after the Bikini Atoll in the Pacific – the site of a nuclear bomb test in 1946 – because he hoped its impact would be as explosive. Legendary fashion editor Diana Vreeland can only have helped him in his mission when she famously proclaimed it was 'the most important thing since the atomic bomb'.

Fashion designers adored the daring two-piece. Back in 1944, Tina Leser's two-piece bathing suits were 'the most daring attire to appear on American beaches to date,' or so declared the photography magazine *Click*. 'Scanty swimsuits are designed to give the girls a maximum of vitamin D and the boys an eyeful.' But it wasn't until Brigitte Bardot was photographed wearing a bikini on a beach in the south of France that the two-piece became a commercial sensation. Roger Vadim is sometimes credited with bringing Brigitte Bardot to Cannes, and it was here in 1953, at the age of 19, that she posed on the sand during the film festival.

Bardot's bikini looks quite demure to modern eyes. But the constructed bandeau and strong horizontal waistline below the navel were the definition of extreme beachwear in the early 1950s. The combination of the starlet, the bikini and the venue worked a kind of magic that clings to the Cannes Film Festival even today.

The bikini was to become the favourite fashion statement of the body beautiful, a garment that would fundamentally change the face of fashion. As Mrs Vreeland remarked, it was 'a swoonsuit that exposed everything about a girl except her mother's maiden name'. In the postwar years this was strong and intoxicating stuff.

Brigitte Bardot single-handedly made the bikini a must-have fashion item, and St-Tropez the bikini-posing capital of the world! This picture was taken in view of a US warship with a full crew of sailors on board. There were no reports of adverse effects on crew or ship. But the Catholic Church reportedly issued flyers ordering the faithful not to watch Bardot's films.

SALVATORE FERRAGAMO

Italian style

Born into poverty in 1898 in the south of Italy, Salvatore Ferragamo qualified as a shoemaker and moved to the USA at the age of 16. He started making shoes for Hollywood in 1923, working on costumes for Cecil B. DeMille. But his business grew out of an increasing demand among the stars for off-duty shoes. Lillian Gish and Mary Pickford were among his first customers.

In 1929, Ferragamo returned to Italy where eventually the privations of World War II were to propel him to stardom as a great design innovator. In the absence of leather, he used cellophane, fish skin and canvas for the uppers of cork-soled shoes. When the steel to support the shanks of high-heeled shoes became unobtainable, he devised wedge heels.

The 1950s were Ferragamo's decade. Italy was becoming a mecca for style and fashion, and attracted tourists from all over the world. There was a booming film industry in Rome's Cinecittà Studios, and this brought the world's greatest and most glamorous stars to his doorstep. And he made shoes for them all. He produced 70 pairs for Greta Garbo, made an annual spring order for the Duchess of Windsor, and created a ballerina for Audrey Hepburn that is still part of the label's classic collection today.

By the time of his death in 1960 he had retail stores in most of the major cities of the world. His showmanship made him one of fashion's most enduring stars. But his commercial success was built on a deep understanding of the physiology of the foot, and on his ability to deliver comfort with style.

Salvatore Ferragamo was one of the few designers who patented his ideas, and he patented every design that could be produced in multiples. The postwar years of economic recovery were especially prolific. In those days it was the designer, not the design team who reigned supreme. In total, Ferragamo created more than 20,000 models of footwear and took out 350 patents.

FIONA CAMPBELL-WALTER

Vogue's 'most beautiful' model

In 1954 Fiona Campbell-Walter was at the peak of her relatively short career and the height of her influence. Audrey Hepburn was admittedly better known and more widely copied after her role in *Sabrina*, but it was Campbell-Walter who was hailed as *Vogue*'s 'most beautiful' model.

Born in Auckland, New Zealand, on 25 June 1932, she first shot to stardom in Britain, where the 'society girl' was a popular heroine and Campbell-Walter was adored because she played the part to perfection. She made an impact in her career as the model who could wear tweeds or the grandest ball gowns with equal elegance. A beauty of thoroughbred purity, she was as intimidating a role model for women of 'normal' proportions then as contemporary supermodels are now.

The wardrobes of Christina Hendricks and January Jones in *Mad Men* are celebrated for their comparative accessibility to 'real women'. But it is interesting to note that few real women could emulate Fiona Campbell-Walter's proportions without the aid of a suffocating corset and highly engineered bra. At a time when Elizabeth Taylor and Gina Lollobrigida were among stars rumoured to have had ribs removed to achieve a hand-span waist, Fiona Campbell-Walter's was entirely natural.

She was whisked into marriage and retirement by one of the richest men in Europe, Baron Hans Heinrich Thyssen-Bornemisza de Kászon, who made her his third wife. The couple married in 1956, and she followed the path of many of her peers into aristocratic anonymity. She resurfaced again only briefly, when her affair with Aristotle Onassis's son Alexandre hit the scandal sheets.

Fiona Campbell-Walter (left), here photographed with Ann Gunning, could command daily fees of up to £2,000: an extortionate amount in the 1950s. Cecil Beaton claimed her as his favourite model, while another photographer gushed: 'Her skin wouldn't support make-up, she was so fresh and beautiful, with that marvellous profile and great allure.'

JEANS

A new American aesthetic

Looking back from the vantage point of 1969, William Burroughs wrote: 'Jack Kerouac was responsible for selling a million pairs of jeans with *On the Road*.' It didn't seem to matter that none of the cast of characters in Kerouac's 1957 manifesto for the Beat Movement actually wore jeans at the time. It was more that with his book the writer gave birth to a new American aesthetic in which the ubiquity of denim became inevitable.

Of course, jeans were part of the American fashion vocabulary before Kerouac. In the Midwest they were the uniform of the cowboy, the all-American hero. In California, jeans were standard issue for the miners as well as for the wild boys who tinkered with their Harley-Davidsons and who were romanticized on screen by Marlon Brando in *The Wild One* (1953).

In New York, jeans were a staple part of the uniform for counter-culture heroes and intellectuals. Roy Lichtenstein and Bob Dylan gave them cool East Coast cred. Even though Elvis is considered a denim icon, it was Eddie Cochrane who really made them rock 'n' roll. Growing up in Mississippi, where jeans were the ordinary clothes of the sharecropper, Elvis never thought them right for the stage. Eddie grew up in Minnesota where they didn't carry the same stigma.

It was Marilyn Monroe who would give denim the stamp of glamour, by wearing Levi jeans and Lee's Storm Rider, the blanket-lined 101J jacket with corduroy collar, on the set of *The Misfits* (1961). France was Levi's first major European market, with Brigitte Bardot frequently seen in 501s.

By the 1950s, jeans had spread beyond their original California heartland, and the selection of denim products had expanded. Denim built up an elusive cachet, becoming a badge of cool. Producer Stanley Kramer's movie *The Wild One* inspired a generation of biker rebels.

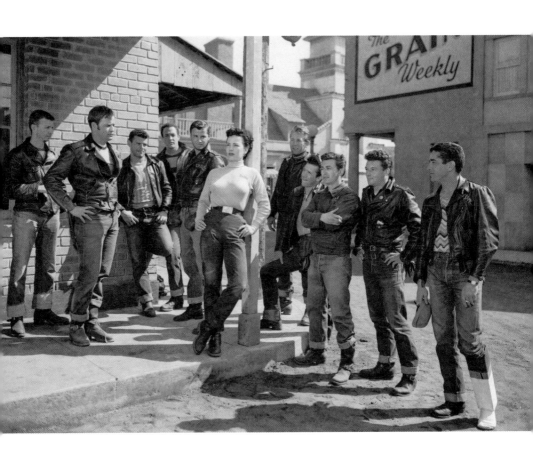

THE CORONATION DRESS

Norman Hartnell designs for Queen Elizabeth II

1953

The high watermark of Norman Hartnell's career was undoubtedly Queen Elizabeth II's coronation gown. It was one of the most important dresses of the twentieth century. What is often forgotten, however, is that it was singlehandedly responsible for turning London into a design centre, and enabling it if not to rival Paris, then at least to challenge its supremacy.

For before Norman Hartnell (1908–75), British designers such as Charles Worth and Edward Molyneux moved their operations to Paris. Those who chose to stay at home found their style somewhat curtailed by a market that was more concerned with its country pursuits and whose leisure time revolved around grand, but chilly houses. Their international reputation was built upon the creation of finely tailored, but rather serviceable tweeds

The Paris couture industry was supported by a vast sub-industry of ateliers that sewed on beading and feathers. It was a system that was much less evolved in London, and yet the coronation dress is considered to be one of the most lavishly decorated of the era. 'I thought of lilies, roses, marguerites and golden corn,' Hartnell wrote in his autobiography. 'I thought of altar clothes and sacred vestments; I thought of the sky, the earth, the sun, the moon, the stars and everything heavenly that might be embroidered on a dress destined to be historic.'

The Queen had requested that Hartnell base the silhouette on that of her wedding gown. The final gown was the eighth design, and was embroidered with floral emblems of each country in the United Kingdom – shamrocks, thistles, Tudor roses, Welsh leeks, oak leaves and acorns. It also included the lotus flower of Ceylon, the South African protea, the Canadian maple leaf and the silver fern of New Zealand. The designer added an extra four-leaf shamrock on the left side of her dress as an omen of good fortune that the Queen's left hand would touch often throughout the day. When she tried it on, the Queen declared it to be 'glorious'.

Millions watched the ceremony on television – for many their first experience of the new medium.

Hartnell submitted eight ideas that started with 'almost severe simplicity and proceeded towards elaboration'. The ultimate design included the emblems of Britain and the Commonwealth. By the time of the coronation Hartnell had 350 employees, and every detail was created by hand in his studio, taking nine weeks and 3,000 man-hours to complete.

MARILYN MONROE
William Travilla dresses the decade's sex goddess

Gentlemen Prefer Blondes (1953) was Marilyn Monroe's breakthrough movie. She proved herself to be an accomplished singer and dancer, and an actress with skilful comic timing. And overnight, the world gained its most famous blonde bombshell.

Shot in vibrant colour, the movie dazzles in every way, not least because of Monroe's voluptuous curves, draped in William Travilla's amazing gowns. Marilyn's costumes, especially the one in which she sings 'Diamonds Are a Girl's Best Friend', were actually intended to be more revealing, but the studio got cold feet. In the wardrobe fittings, executives caught one glimpse of her pneumatic figure draped in spangled fishnet and asked Travilla to cover her up. It hardly mattered. Even in long gloves and an ankle-length gown, an iconic sex symbol was born.

Marilyn dominated the movie, with that unique combination of sensuality and innocence that became the hallmark of her fame. She is recognized by many as a trailblazer for the sexual revolution because of the way she sold her sensuality, pushing the boundaries of public acceptance and skirting the limits of approbation. UK cultural commentator Julie Burchill has written, 'She played stupid girls who thought they were smart but she was a smart girl who thought she was stupid.'

The potency of her screen sex goddess image – her halo of platinum curls, her curvaceous figure, her pouting mouth, batting lashes and beauty mark – continues to mesmerize. She has always remained a powerful figure in the popular imagination, inspiring the likes of Madonna, Gwen Stefani and countless impersonators.

Monroe's pink dress was auctioned on 11 June 2010, with an estimated price of between $150,000 and $250,000 and described as 'the most important film costume to ever come to auction'. It sold for $310,000. Paradoxically, considering her role in the movie as a blonde 'mantrap', in real life she was the least materialistic of Hollywood stars.

TEENAGERS
The decade's dominant fashion force

The 1950s saw a radical demographic shift, and with it arrived the 'teenager'. Teenagers set a new agenda, distancing themselves from the world of adults. They had cash from paid work, or pocket money from newly affluent parents, and a strong sense of their own style. They took their lead from popular culture: rock 'n' roll idols such as Elvis Presley, Bill Hayley and Jerry Lee Lewis and film stars like James Dean and Marlon Brando.

Teenage style was expressed through its own music, cafés and even forms of transportation (scooters became the vehicle of choice). Fashion news spread fast, as television and fashion magazines documented and disseminated every emerging trend. In these early days of youth culture, America led and European teenagers followed.

Tribes such as 'greasers' and 'preppies' inspired dogged loyalty. Greasers were the denim- and biker-jacketed rebels who took their cue from Marlon Brando in *The Wild One* (1953). It was a bonus, of course, that the conservative older generation found them terrifying. Preppies, on the other hand, were paragons of neatness. A preppie teen wardrobe ranged from full dirndl or sunray-pleated skirt to T-shirts and sweaters with large appliqués. Tight-fitting blouses tucked into 'Capri' pants or 'pedal pushers', short ankle socks, scarves tied around the neck and cropped cardigans completed the preppie look.

As new role models sprang weekly from the movie theatre and record store, revolutionary fabrics such as polyester and spandex made it faster and easier to get their look. By the end of the decade, teenage fashion had emerged as a huge industry. Teenagers were suddenly a dominant force and a marketing man's dream.

Here eighteen-year-old Italian actress Elsa Martinelli (on the set of her first film *Le Rouge et la Noir*) shows how keenly European youth was influenced by US teenage style.

THE FIRST CHANEL SUIT

Coco's comeback classic

At the outbreak of World War II, Gabrielle 'Coco' Chanel (1883–1971) was already a fashion superstar. By loosening the corseted silhouette and commandeering unorthodox fabrics such as the jersey used for men's underwear, she had made a name for herself. Her 'look' started with her own wardrobe and lifestyle. With her tanned skin, financial independence and boyish figure, she was the living embodiment of the Chanel fashion ideal and an early example of the power of personality in fashion marketing.

Having established her headquarters at 31, rue Cambon in Paris (where the Chanel fashion house remains to this day), she closed when Germany invaded France.

She railed against fashion's first postwar hit: Dior's New Look. In her eyes, that corseted silhouette with its nipped-in waist and full skirt was an affront to the liberated women who had played such vital and active roles during the war. It was the antithesis of everything she stood for. In much the same way as she had done following World War I, Chanel saw it as her mission to rescue and reinvigorate women's fashion.

Her comeback was not an instant critical success. But her collection for Winter 1954 saw the launch of her reworking of her classic tweeds in the form of the Chanel suit. With its slim skirt and collarless jacket trimmed in braid with gold buttons, patch pockets, and – sewn into the hem – a gold-coloured chain, which together ensured a perfect line from the shoulder, it became a status symbol for a new generation and remains a classic to this day.

In 1954 Chanel was goaded into action because, she said, 'there are too many men in this business, and they don't know how to make clothes for women. How can a woman wear a dress that's cut so she can't lift up her arm to pick up a telephone?' Her famous suit was an enormous hit.

AUDREY HEPBURN IN *SABRINA*

Hepburn meets Givenchy and one of fashion's longest collaborations begins

Audrey Hepburn's collaboration with Givenchy started with the film *Sabrina* (1954) and caused an earthquake among the style conscious. Like Coco Chanel, she not only changed the way women dressed but also altered forever the way they viewed themselves, broadening the definition of beauty and offering the world a less submissive, less blatantly sexual model than the pinups of the day.

Every woman wanted to be Audrey Hepburn (1929–93). The embrace of Audrey's style went further than the clothes on her back. 'Everyone on the street was copying Audrey's hair,' Dreda Mele, *directrice* of Givenchy at the time, recalled, 'the way she moved, the way she spoke. They copied her for ten solid years after.'

Hubert de Givenchy's name is missing from the credits on *Sabrina* because credit was contractually bound to go to Edith Head, the famed costume designer at Paramount (see page 56), who at the time also tried to take the plaudits for Givenchy's 'décolleté Sabrina'. In spite of this tricky start, the movie marked the beginning of Hollywood's longest-running wardrobe collaboration.

Givenchy designed Hepburn's wardrobe for *Funny Face*, *Love in the Afternoon*, *Breakfast at Tiffany's*, *Charade*, *Paris When It Sizzles* and *How to Steal a Million*. He also designed her dress for her second wedding and her sons' christening gowns. Together they developed the crisp lines, simple colour and extraordinary workmanship that defined Audrey's style – described by the Spanish shoe designer Manolo Blahnik as 'the most important look of the twentieth century'.

Givenchy confirmed that Audrey's elevation to global style leader was no accident: 'She knew exactly what she wanted. She, moreover, knew perfectly her body's fine points and faults: she wanted a bare-shouldered evening dress modified to hide the hollows behind her collarbone. What I invented for her eventually became a style so popular that I named it the décolleté Sabrina.'

Hepburn's style was of a subtle grown-up kind for the newly style-conscious America that would in a few short years embrace the heady optimism of Camelot, the Kennedys and the 1960s. Billy Wilder, the director and producer of *Sabrina*, picked up on her sophisticated appeal, saying, 'This girl, singlehandedly, may make bosoms a thing of the past.'

HUBERT DE GIVENCHY
The aristocratic designer

The aristocratic Hubert de Givenchy (1927–) arrived in Paris at the age of 17 to work with Jacques Fath and to realize his childhood dream to be a dress designer. By the time he set up his own house in 1952, he had added experience with Robert Piguet, Lucien Lelong and Elsa Schiaparelli to his CV.

The house of Givenchy debuted with a collection that included the Bettina blouse, named after his PR director and model of the day, Bettina Graziani (see page 24). It was a look that was to be a Givenchy signature for the length of his career. The blouse was made from the raw cotton 'shirting' that had previously been used only for couture fittings.

It wasn't long before Givenchy was attracting notable clients. Indeed, during more than 40 years as a couturier he dressed some of the most memorable women of the century. Grace Kelly wore an emerald-green Givenchy on her first official visit to President Kennedy in Washington, DC in 1961. He created the wardrobe for Jackie Kennedy's state visit to France in the same year, and in 1972 the Duchess of Windsor wore a black coat by Givenchy to her husband's funeral.

But it was his association with Audrey Hepburn (see page 50) that was to last the longest and be the most influential. Givenchy designed the black sheath dress that the actress wore in *Breakfast at Tiffany's* (1961), as well as costumes for the films *Sabrina*, *Charade* and *Funny Face*, and clothes for her off-screen life.

When the pair first met, Givenchy was expecting an encounter with the then much more famous Katharine Hepburn. However, when Audrey turned up dressed in a knotted T-shirt, flat sandals and a gondolier's hat, they discovered an instant rapport that was to lead to lifelong friendship between the aristocratic designer and his muse.

Givenchy dispensed with the boning, padding and stuffing that characterized the competition. His was a simpler approach: separates that could be worn together or in a variety of combinations. No big deal today, but his uncomplicated and young style was revolutionary in its time – and a huge success. On the first day of selling, Givenchy Couture was reported to have racked up sales of seven million francs.

C Z GUEST

Patrician East Coast chic

'She came into the bar of the Ritz wearing a knee-length tweed skirt, a twinset and moccasins – and in a time when everyone else was tarted up in Dior's New Look, she stopped traffic,' remembered designer Bill Blass of C Z Guest (1920–2003).

She was the archetypal WASP ice blonde, an impeccably raised young lady and an accomplished horsewoman who competed all over America, but who nevertheless ran away to become a showgirl in Darryl Zanuck's Ziegfeld Follies and was painted nude by Diego Rivera. She put her early years behind her when, in 1947, she married Winston Guest on Hemingway's plantation in Cuba. She was an unassuming style icon. Commenting on her role as a designer muse, she said, 'I like fitted clothes that show off the body. I wasn't the inspiration for Mainbocher. My style was his style.'

Early in the 1950s, the New York Dress Institute cited her as one of the best-dressed women in the world, and she remained on the list for years until her elevation to the Fashion Hall of Fame. *Time* magazine had her photographed by Horst for the cover of an issue in 1962 that ran with the headline 'A Legend in Her Own Time'.

Her look was classic American thoroughbred: honey blonde hair, pale complexion and a slim athletic figure dressed in simple lines, luxurious fabrics and a combination of neutral and fondant pastel colours. Her unfussy, clean-cut style defined the archetypical patrician American look. Her style is the foundation on which Grace Kelly built a career and Ralph Lauren an empire. It became the blueprint of acceptability in the enclaves of Palm Beach and Southampton: a sporty, outdoorsy look that eschewed make-up, hairspray and, heaven forfend, anything resembling a trend.

C Z Guest stands out among Truman Capote's fabled 'swans' as the smoothest of the flock. The 'cool vanilla lady', as he called her, had an 'ice cream reserve' that measured up to her sartorial discipline. 'She dreads overdressing,' *Vogue* observed in 1959. Here she poses with Joanne Connolly (right) beside the Grecian temple pool of her Palm Beach estate.

EDITH HEAD

Pillar of the Hollywood studio
system and American fashion

Edith Head (1897–1981) was the fabled costume designer who worked for Paramount Pictures for 43 years. She was Hitchcock's favourite costume designer; she created Dorothy Lamour's famous sarong dress, and she also dressed Audrey Hepburn in *Roman Holiday* (1953).

But the gossip in Hollywood was that Paramount's formidable doyenne of the costume department wasn't a designer at all. Detractors dismissed her as 'the queen of the shirtwaisters'. It was said she didn't even know how to draw. She admitted to getting her first job interview with someone else's sketches, and it was rumoured that she continued to add her distinctive looping signature at the bottom of others' work. She controversially got credit for Givenchy's work with Audrey Hepburn, claiming the 'décolleté Sabrina' as her own, having in reality designed only the ragamuffin, living-over-the-garage costumes in the movie.

While her design credentials may have been suspect, she was nonetheless an accomplished handler of people. In the hierarchical studio system, Edith was famous for being the only person who could be both 'subservient and behave like a star'. Leading Hollywood ladies such as Ginger Rogers, Shirley MacLaine, Barbara Stanwyck, Elizabeth Taylor and Natalie Wood demanded to work with her. In a world full of prima donnas, Head had the hardnosed acumen of a corporate executive. She subtly made herself indispensable to those above her in the power chain. Whenever a star or an important executive's wife needed to borrow a dress to go to a premiere or a party at Romanoff's, Edith happily lent them something.

Head is immortalized as the firebrand Edna Mode in Pixar's 2004 cartoon feature *The Incredibles*.

During her 58-year career, Head received more than a thousand screen credits, won 35 Oscar nominations, and got the Academy Award for costume design an unprecedented eight times. Her ability to placate difficult personalities and to camouflage problem figures made her a huge success and a Hollywood legend.

GRACE KELLY
The ideal 1950s blonde

Grace Kelly (1929–82) was the perfect 1950s beauty. She did not necessarily lead fashion, but she became a byword for an impeccably polished look.

It was New York fashion designer Oleg Cassini, briefly engaged to Kelly, who claimed to have created the Kelly look, but it was the director Alfred Hitchcock who honed it. Even the mighty costume mistress Edith Head admits she deferred to the director's vision. The director was obsessed with creating Kelly as a 'credible hybrid of elegance and sex'. And the pastel shades and pristine white that he believed best suited his ideal blonde became her signature.

Even in mufti, dressed, as Cassini described her, 'like a school teacher' in her wool skirts, cashmere cardies and horn-rimmed glasses, she had 'a white-gloved glow'. She had studied ballet and never lost a dancer's awareness of her limbs and posture. Her unique walk became part of her style: regal above the waist and floating below, it was compared to a geisha's glide.

Hitchcock and Kelly understood the appealing edge added by the conflict implicit in her style. At once ladylike and elemental, it carried beneath its ice-cool exterior a suggestion of something more passionate. Her remoteness on screen became a reality when, after a fleeting five years of Hollywood fame, she disappeared to marry Prince Rainier and join a European royal family.

And yet she was down to earth with a reserved, bluestocking style. Brought up in a disciplined and conservative household, even at the height of her Hollywood fame she eschewed couture. It didn't stop her making joint number one on the 1955 'best dressed' list, alongside socialite Babe Paley who dressed in Mainbocher. Her likeness, that year, was used to create a line of mannequins.

In *To Catch a Thief* (1955), Kelly's gowns were based on classical draping, with sheer trains and scarves creating wafting breezes around her neck. Reflecting the Hellenistic sculpting of 1950s couturier Mme Grès, they gave Kelly the allure of an earthbound goddess. Fitted bodices and billowing skirts in a palette of pastel and white were a quintessentially Kelly-esque fusion of the balletic and the sporty.

SOPHIA LOREN
Italian bombshell glamour

The Italian bombshell of the 1950s was a reluctant style icon. Sophia Loren (1934–) made it through a rough, poverty-stricken childhood, and as an aspiring beauty queen was discovered in Rome by film producer Carlo Ponti, the man who would later became her husband.

She became the benchmark of Italian bombshell glamour throughout the 50s and 60s. No one has ever worn a corset with the same sophisticated and sizzling aplomb as Sophia Loren in *Marriage Italian Style* (1964). And, now well into her seventies, she continues to inspire the red-carpet style of contemporary starlets. There is more than a soupçon of Sophia in the likes of Scarlett Johansson and Eva Mendes. An Italian national treasure and a fashion inspiration, she remains a front-row presence at Giorgio Armani and Valentino fashion shows.

Loren is quoted as saying, 'Everything you see, I owe to spaghetti.' And even though she has denied ever having said this, it was indeed her curvaceous figure and seductive joie de vivre that catapulted her to global stardom. Her voluptuous figure was a constant reminder that her first stage name was 'Sofia Lazzaro' – as it was claimed her beauty could raise men from the dead.

Dolce & Gabbana's Summer 2012 collection was dedicated to the image of Loren in *Pane, amore e …* (1955). The scoop-necked dresses with nipped-in waists and full skirts in sunny summer prints, accessorized with straw baskets, stilettoes and headscarves, were pure Sophia.

'A woman's dress should be like a barbed-wire fence,' Loren once declared, 'serving its purpose without obstructing the view.'

Sophia Loren burned up the silver screen to become the epitome of the Cinecittà sex symbol. In the comedy *Pane, amore e …* she played a lovely fishmonger with an unfeasibly gorgeous wardrobe. Circling her seventieth birthday, she was placed sixth in *Playboy*'s 100 Sexiest Women of the Century.

BEATNIK STYLE
Art delinquents who believed the pen is mightier than the sword

The new youth culture movements of the 1950s tended to take root first among the working classes. However, the beatniks who emerged in America and Europe during the middle of the decade were firmly entrenched in the middle class.

Beatniks rebelled against the establishment and their parents. They shored up the generation gap, questioning not only their own upbringing but also authority, the government, the arms race and all bastions of middle-class affluence. In America, the Beat movement thrived in New York in the Greenwich Village bars and coffeehouses where the acolytes of writers Jack Kerouac and William Burroughs gathered. In Paris they gravitated to the company of philosopher Jean-Paul Sartre and chanteuse Juliette Greco in the cafés of St-Germain-des-Prés.

The Beat Generation were the early precursors of the hippie movement, producing a culture of dropping out from society and rejecting its familiar touchstones. Dropouts need a uniform to set themselves apart from society, and their particular sartorial statement was made in head-to-toe black. It was described as a combination of the 'French bohemian, English intellectual and US hobo'. They wore polo necks and jeans, duffel coats and dark glasses. They were art delinquents who loved jazz and poetry, who believed the pen was mightier than the sword. They were immortalized on screen in glorious VistaVision by the Audrey Hepburn character in the 1957 film *Funny Face*.

Journalist Lee Gibb commented: 'They have replaced the American haircut with the French haircut. They have replaced high heels by low heels, low heels by no heels and no heels by bare feet.'

The idealism of Kerouac became a fashion statement thanks to Audrey Hepburn in *Funny Face*. Writer Joyce Johnson defined its value to the marketing men when she said, 'the "Beat Generation" sold books, black turtleneck sweaters and bongos, berets and dark glasses, sold a way of life that seemed like dangerous fun.'

EASY-CARE FABRICS

Space age technology produces miracle yarns

With post–World War II economic expansion came a new generation of synthetic fabrics. In the summer of 1952 the term 'wash and wear' was coined to describe a new blend of cotton and acrylic. The 'easy-care' fabric family was to grow and grow.

Acrylic was marketed alongside nylon and other synthetics as a 'miracle fabric' – crease-proof, shrink-proof and quick-drying. 'Drip-dry' nylon and Dacron could retain heat-set pleats after washing, and became immensely popular. Polyester came along in 1953, offering a fabric that would keep its shape in spite of the most brutal crushing and which did not wrinkle with everyday wear. A tagline from an Orlon advertisement stresses the uncreasability of the DuPont acrylic, showing an impeccably dressed mother in New Look silhouette greeting her family off a plane: 'With Orlon you hide the miles you've traveled.'

The clothing industry went into creative overdrive with the new design possibilities presented by the new materials. By the mid-1950s a boom in women's knitwear was under way, and acrylic, perfectly suited to imitate expensive wool, was there to meet the demand. By the 1960s sales were worth £1 million a year.

The availability of synthetic fibres profoundly influenced the way Americans and Europeans clothed themselves and lived. Women had to handle the family wash at home. Synthetics made that not just easier but in many cases possible. The new fibres also represented a trade-off – they were easier to iron and longer lasting, but harder to keep clean and uncomfortable for some uses (shirts and underwear, for example).

Wrinkle-resistant and durable, synthetic fibres were embraced by a culture that equated crisp clothing and neat home furnishings with bourgeois respectability.

The dream wardrobe of the future was available in the present to middle-class consumers with increasing spending power. Mass clothing manufacturers made lavish and creative use of 'miracle fibres' to produce fashion that a generation before would have been beyond the reach of all but the wealthiest.

now: jersey you can wash and wear! It's 100%

ACRILAN

Machine-wash (or hand-wash if you prefer). Use a warm-water setting; drip-dry. Pleats
stay crisp, shape will stay luscious with little if any ironing. Rich to see and feel, too: *this*
jersey's 100% Acrilan acrylic fiber! *styled by Kay Busgang for* ALICE STUART

BRIGITTE BARDOT
A sensuous idol

In the pantheon of legendary blondes, Brigitte Bardot (1934–) reigns at the right hand of Marilyn Monroe. She took the ingredients of the classic 1950s heroine, the breathless, wide-eyed, innocent blonde, and put a flirtatious French spin on her. *Vogue* called her 'the sensuous idol, a potent mixture of the sexy and the babyish, a seething milky bosom below a childish pout'. The phrase 'sex kitten' was coined to describe her.

She captured the imagination of intellectuals and film fans alike. The French feminist Simone de Beauvoir described her as 'a locomotive of women's history' and declared her the first and most liberated woman of postwar France. She became a national treasure, and in 1969 was chosen to model for the face of Marianne, a previously anonymous figure representing the state of France.

Born in 1934, Bardot was the embodiment of a new carefree, laissez-faire lifestyle. She made her home in St-Tropez, thereby putting that small fishing village on the fashion map. St-Tropez typified the lifestyle she embodied – one of scruffy insouciance and spontaneous chic – and, having received the benediction of the luminaries of the Nouvelle Vague, it gave birth to trends that were adopted on beaches around the world. Thanks to Bardot, the bikini became a global, barnstorming fashion success.

She enjoyed the heady existence that typified the time. She started as a model and a dancer, appearing on the pages of French *Elle* at 15 and enrolling at the Conservatoire nationale de danse in Paris before becoming an actress. The elements of her style were a polka-dot scarf, short shorts, a full-skirted gingham dress, a sweep of eyeliner and the 'choucroute' hairstyle. The Bardot neckline (a wide open sweep that reveals the shoulders) is a recurring catwalk detail that to this day signals her enduring fashion influence.

She was one of the few European actresses of the 1950s and 60s to achieve success in the United States. Idolized by public and stars alike (including John Lennon, Paul McCartney and Bob Dylan), she was propelled to fame by her 'sex kitten' image. In 1956 her role in *Et Dieu ... créa la femme* pushed the limits of censorship in America, and her ever-increasing army of fans loved it.

FRANÇOISE SAGAN
The 'charming little monster'

During the 1950s Françoise Sagan (1935–2004) became a star, expressing all the rebelliousness of her peers in the French bourgeoisie. A Sorbonne dropout, she famously blew her advance for *Bonjour Tristesse* (1954), her first novel, on a black sweater and rounds of whisky for her friends. The English translation of *Bonjour Tristesse* went to number one in the *New York Times* bestseller list the following year, and in 1958 Otto Preminger directed the movie version starring Jean Seberg.

This meteoric success made Françoise Sagan independently wealthy at the age of 19. And she lived large. With the early proceeds of her first novel she bought a mink coat for her mother and a Jaguar for herself. She drank till dawn and gambled lavishly. It has been reported that she once made a killing at the gaming tables of Deauville and used the money to buy herself a turn-of-the-century chateau. She suffered severe head trauma when she overturned her Aston Martin in 1957.

She was the symbol of fashionable rebellion in postwar Europe. One critic called her 'a notorious representative of the younger generation'. The writer François Mauriac described her as 'a charming little monster'. With her gamine face and her thirst for hard liquor, shiny sports cars and thrilling sex, Ms Sagan resembled a sensuous tomboy. Her life in the 1950s was one long lunch, drinking and carousing session with the likes of Tennessee Williams, Henry Miller, Roger Vadim, Jean-Luc Godard and Juliette Greco.

She was the archetype of the teenage rebel in a postwar Paris that was electric with beatniks, jazz and existentialism. She articulated teenage angst with unique style: like a literary Keith Richards, she was a breath of fresh air in the hyper-bourgeois France of the 1950s.

GRACE KELLY'S WEDDING DRESS

One of the most copied gowns of all time

1956

It was dubbed the 'Wedding of the Century'. Grace Kelly referred privately to it as the 'Carnival of the Century'. Whichever way you look at it, the wedding of Prince Rainier of Monaco and Grace Kelly on 19 April 1956 in Monaco cathedral, watched by 30 million people, was arguably the first multimedia event on a modern scale.

The gown Grace Kelly wore is one of the most copied wedding dresses of all time. More than 50 years later, commentators noted that, at another wedding of the century, Kate Middleton's dress by Sarah Burton for Alexander McQueen had distinct 'echoes of Grace Kelly's style'.

At the Monaco wedding, nearly two thousand reporters and photographers were present to record the picture-perfect ideal of postwar 1950s culture. Even the pink cathedral atop its white steps looked like a Marguerite Patten cake. Grace walked up the aisle watched by guests including Ava Gardner, François Mitterrand and Jean Cocteau.

It was a ceremony of epic Hollywood proportions, with a wardrobe to match. Little wonder – given that, in exchange for the termination of her contract, she had granted MGM exclusive rights to produce *The Wedding in Monaco*, a half-hour documentary chronicling the nuptials. The studio bankrolled the extravagant Monte Carlo wedding and also paid for the wedding dress.

However, Grace's own attitude hinted at the conflict that would define her future life as a public figure exposed to almost continuous and intrusive scrutiny. As Prince Rainier himself said, 'Grace would have loved to run off and be married in a simple little chapel in the mountains. This unrealistic idea really enchanted me.'

The dress – 25 yards of silk taffeta, antique rose-point lace and pearls – was created by Helen Rose, an MGM costume designer. It was she who had dressed Kelly in safari chic for *Mogambo* (1953) and in the memorable fit-and-flare looks of *High Society* (1956).

70

THE KELLY BAG

Fashion's most enduring 'It' bag

It was the director Alfred Hitchcock who was behind fashion's first ever 'It' bag. For it was he who suggested to costume designer Edith Head that she go to Hermès in Paris to buy accessories for the 1954 movie *To Catch a Thief*. Of their visit to the Faubourg St-Honoré store, Head recalled that she and Grace Kelly 'were like two girls in an ice cream shop. We fell in love with everything we saw.'

The boxy handbag that was Kelly's favourite was to become the icon of the house that endures today. It was a descendant of the 1930s Hermès saddlebag (the *sac à dépêches pour dames*) that was originally called the *haut à courroies*. But two years later, in 1956, Hermès rechristened it, after Princess Grace used a version in brown pigskin to hide her pregnancy from prying paparazzi. The photograph appeared in *Life* magazine and the phenomenon of 'the Kelly' was born.

Simple and yet impeccably made, in small production runs, by craftsmen in the Hermès factory, the bag rapidly achieved iconic, 'must-have' fashion status. The Birkin, Hermès' other bestselling bag, may have an element of showy glamour about it, but, by contrast the Kelly remains an understated classic – the bag that has played a supporting role to stylish women of all ages for more than 80 years. Despite a prohibitive price starting at £3,500, there are long waiting lists at Hermès stores around the world for the opportunity to buy one.

To this day, only one craftsperson, who may have been employed by the company for decades, makes a single handbag at a time, hand-stitching individual pieces with linen thread and an awl. One bag might take 18 to 24 hours to produce. Waiting lists remain predictably long.

JAYNE MANSFIELD

Blonde ambition

Jayne Mansfield (1933–67) was frequently branded a poor man's Marilyn Monroe. Certainly the blonde bombshell from Pennsylvania lived up to the stereotype she helped to create. But while she may have been the archetypical Hollywood blonde, her style gives clues to more intriguing contradictions.

Swathed in figure-clinging dresses and tight-fitting sweaters, and with arms and ears piled up with paste costume jewellery, she was unmissable. Her hair was peroxide-white blonde and her lips were extravagantly red. So far so ditsy, but she was far greater than the sum of her eye-popping parts. With an IQ of 163, she was a proficient musician and an actress with a flair for comedic timing.

In a world where women were paragons of pastel-dressed perfection, Jayne was bold, brash and modern, with a daredevil spirit. She was also a crusading self-promoter. She was a head-turning presence, but if she startled she also inspired, and the classic 1950s silhouette of curvaceous slim waist and underwired 'missile' bosom was all Mansfield.

She saw her main rival as Marilyn Monroe, another curvaceous blonde. But their personalities and looks were quite different. Jayne was more confident about her looks and would use them to get publicity and attention. She happily traded on her figure and sexuality, becoming Hollywood's first onscreen nude. She cheerfully went out in public in see-through dresses that scandalized audiences. One appearance was in a leopard-print bikini, accessorized by her Mr Universe husband, Mickey Hargitay, dressed as Tarzan.

Mansfield defined 1950s extravagance and decadence. Larger than life, she was a caricature of the blonde starlets of the era. However, she was also one of 1950s Tinseltown's biggest phenomena.

In the years 1956 and 1957 Mansfield's photo was published on separate occasions in more than 2,500 newspapers. She was a household name and was frequently compared to Marilyn Monroe. In response to this she was quoted as saying, 'Cleavage, of course, helped me get to where I am. I don't know how she got there.'

THE JET SET

London for breakfast, New York for lunch

Travel opened up after the war, although not for everyone. In the 1950s, the new jet passenger services were primarily marketed to the rich. The 'jet set' was a group of wealthy people whose busy social diaries included engagements in chic and rarefied locations all over the world. Their lifestyles were glamorous and stratospherically beyond the reach of the majority, whose lives revolved around the daily commute and weekend socializing in the suburbs.

The new jet set were the children of the café society, freed to travel from one fabulously stylish place to another by the jet aircraft. BOAC inaugurated the first commercial scheduled jet service on 2 May 1952, from London to New York. As other routes opened up, so too did the diaries of the jet set. Other cities on the standard jet set routes were Paris, Rome and Los Angeles. Jet set resorts such as Acapulco, Nassau and Bermuda flourished, while the formerly sleepy towns of St-Tropez, Capri and Cannes became the busy hubs of the social universe.

The original members of this elite group of glamorous global nomads were socialites who were not shy of publicity, and whose nightly entertainments took place in semi-public places such as nightclubs and restaurants, where the 'paparazzi' – another jet set phenomenon – photographed them. They were fantastically aspirational figures: superstars of the first generation who might weekend in Paris or fly to Rome just for a party. Their lifestyle was memorably captured in Fellini's *La Dolce Vita* (1960).

Long before the advent of budget airlines, passengers dressed for travel. One BOAC flight from Southampton to Johannesburg boasted a lounge/dining area on the upper deck, two dressing rooms on the lower deck, and 'day and night accommodation' for 24 passengers.

ROCKABILLY
'Postwar punk rockers'

Rockabilly, the music of Elvis, Buddy Holly and Bill Haley and one of the earliest forms of rock 'n' roll, emerged early in the decade. The name is a hybrid of 'rock ['n' roll]' and 'hillbilly', a reference to country music (which was often called hillbilly music in the 1940s and 50s). The music and the style were inextricably linked.

With the end of World War II and prosperity on the rise, young people had the opportunity for the first time to create identities that had nothing to do with the generation that had gone before. Their parents might have needed to get jobs to support their families, but young people in the 1950s had much more free time on their hands. Youth culture had arrived. Some stayed on longer at school. But the clean-cut preppie was the polar opposite of the rebellious rockabilly youth. They were menacing, outrageous and frightening: for a sense of their impact, think 'postwar punk rockers' in customized cars or on roaring motorbikes.

Men wore well-greased pompadours (a style that Elvis had copied from the truckers in the Southern states), jeans (a staple of the working man's wardrobe) and tough leather jackets. Women wore wide circular skirts held out with nylon petticoats, scoop-neck blouses, back-to-front cardigans, tight sweaters or polo necks, and three-quarter-sleeve fitted shirts, often with a scarf knotted cowboy fashion at the neck. Both music and fashion were neatly calculated to distance youthful rockabillies from the previous generation.

In Britain, rockabilly fans were called 'Teddy boys' on account of their Edwardian frock-coats, which they wore with black drainpipe jeans and brothel creepers. By the early 1960s, they had morphed into rockers and adopted the classic 'greaser' look of jeans and leather jackets to go with their heavily slicked quiffs.

WILLIAM KLEIN
Fashion's fabulous iconoclast

In the 1950s, photographers and models achieved star status and became household names for the first time. They were heroes of a new popular culture that flourished in magazines. At the same time newspaper editors became more interested in them, and not just for the gossip columns. They realized that fashion pages could be a dynamic and glamorous presence in their papers. And, understanding that men as well as women looked at these features, they started to use the pictures that were a little sexier and more sensational. Photographers began to use models in a more provocative way.

On the cutting edge of this new mood was William Klein (1928–), a young American photographer living in Paris. Through his work he brought an unusually acid and ironic approach to fashion photography. In the world of haute couture, where the haughty froideur of well-born beauties was a given, Klein was an iconoclast.

The edgy environments he chose in which to shoot his fashion stories were as important as the clothes. He managed to capture the qualities of movies and television in his dynamic images. His models looked independent and tough, with a kind of knowing air. They looked streetwise, versed in the rules of the city, not the salon. It was a world away from what qualified as the classic chic of the time. And it set a new standard for fashion photography.

'I used semi-nuts,' he said. 'I liked the tough girls from New York and the backstreets rather than the socialites. In my photos the girls are always in trouble, always askew. Or I play two girls off each other. Helmut Newton's pictures come out of mine because I was the first to use hard girls.'

Klein, the artist turned photographer, has combined a career as a photographer and photojournalist with that of film maker, and his fashion images, such as this, have all the drama of a movie still.

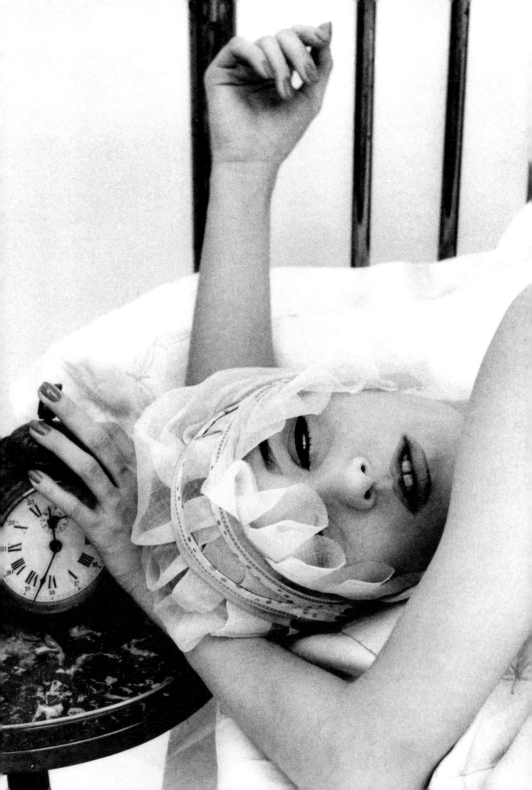

CLARE McCARDELL
The American modernist

1957

After the war years of militaristic suits, armoured shoulder pads and nose-cone breasts, McCardell liberated the women of the 1950s from the strictures of mother's girdle. According to *Vogue*, the ideal Claire McCardell woman was 'a long-legged tennis-playing swimming girl. … She looked exactly like the typical American girl, just as real, only prettier.'

Claire McCardell (1905–58) made clothes that were revolutionary and also right for every girl in America. There was something of the pioneer woman in the frugal but beautiful cut of the suit; something of the workman in the stout welt seaming. McCardell invented things within the limits of mass production at a time of couture. She could take $5 of common cotton and turn out a dress a smart woman could wear anywhere. Her clothes were relatively inexpensive because she used cotton instead of satin and silk.

'Clothes ought to be useful and comfortable,' McCardell said. 'I've often wondered why they had to be delicate – why they couldn't be practical and sturdy as well as feminine.' One of her constants was the monastic dress, which could be full or slim as long as it didn't have a built-in waistline – she preferred her customers to determine where their own waist should be by selling her dresses with tie sashes.

McCardell also created a six-piece interchangeable wardrobe for the woman traveller, with skirt, jacket, blouse, trousers, shorts and halter top in either denim or black butcher cloth. Her inspiration, McCardell claimed, came from solving problems.

The story of American fashion owes much to Claire McCardell, who has been described as having introduced 'the American Look', in contrast to Dior's New Look. The feminist Betty Friedan described her as 'the girl who defied Dior'.

SUZY PARKER

The vivacious face of the 1950s

It was Suzy Parker (1932–2003) who inspired the beatnik character played by Audrey Hepburn in *Funny Face* (1957). She was also the favourite model of the movie's visual consultant, the photographer Richard Avedon. He said she gave modelling 'emotion and reality. She invented the form and no one surpassed her.' She was, he declared, 'the most challenging and complicated' of his muses.

It was Avedon who introduced spirited animation into fashion photography, and it was Parker who realized his vision in front of the camera. She roller-skated in the place de la Concorde for his camera – in a Dior dress of course. Her older sister was Dorian Leigh, a famous model of the 1940s who introduced her, at the tender age of 14, to Eileen Ford. The legendary model agent said of her afterwards: 'She was the most beautiful creature you can imagine; she was everybody's everything.'

Parker travelled to Paris at 17 for *Harper's Bazaar* and stayed on, exploring the Left Bank clad in existential black. Modelling gave her access to anywhere she wanted to go, although she dropped it to become apprentice to photographer Henri Cartier-Bresson and to edit French *Vogue*. But the money was alluring – at $200 an hour she was the highest-paid 'face' of the time. And as the fashion editor Diana Vreeland once remarked, 'Hers was the face of the 50s.'

Parker was an icon for the re-launched house of Chanel. Charles Revson of Revlon cosmetics was obsessed with her, and she was able to demand the exclusive contract that only became commonplace decades later, even though Mr Revson was of the opinion that 'the sheer joy of working for Revlon should be enough'.

Parker was given a cameo in *Funny Face* by its director, Stanley Donen, who also cast her in *Kiss Them for Me* (1957) with Cary Grant and Jayne Mansfield. But she was something of a flop on the big screen: her vivacity did not translate.

'Suzy Parker didn't stop talking when I first tried to take her picture,' recalled, the photographer Horst. 'I said, "You keep talking," and I left. When she got into the movies, I joked that maybe she would do for the movies what she would never do for me – hold still.'

THE GOSSARD CORSET
A girl's best hope of achieving
fashion's impossible ideal

In her 1959 book *Wife Dressing*, the US designer Anne Fogarty advocated wearing a girdle 'with everything' – a practice that she blithely compared with Chinese foot binding. Her 18-inch waist was a great source of personal pride, and her favourite cocktail dresses were the ones that were so structured she could only stand up in them. She felt very strongly that clothes should fit snugly, especially after 5 p.m. 'You are not meant to suffer,' she reassured her readers, but the feeling should 'be one of constraint rather than comfort.'

Nor was she a lone voice in the wilderness. Of all the elements of the New Look silhouette, the waistline was probably at once the most coveted and the most difficult to achieve. Engineered undergarments were critical for the perfect foundation. Dior employed traditional corsetry techniques, but developments in new synthetics made corset-dependent fashion possible for all women. The new contraptions had nicknames like the 'waspie', and could achieve 'quite the tiniest waistline in three decades'. Fashion editors ran pages of advice on how to achieve the almost caricatured femininity that had come to replace the dreary utilitarian wardrobe of the war years.

Contemporary fashion illustrated a key female function of the decade, which was to entertain and attend social gatherings – usually to promote a spouse's career. This new formality is reflected in highly structured garments. *Good Housekeeping* magazine noted at the time that, 'we are going to be feminine with greater accent on a tiny waist, fuller hips, higher heels', and advised: 'like an old-fashioned corselet, a nylon marquisette shrinks your waist and rounds your hip line.'

The ideal was the tiny waist and concave stomach that Nancy White, a fashion columnist at the time, called the 'gasp waist'.

We may well laugh, but foundation garments such as these were fundamental to the way women dressed until well into the 1960s. Nowadays, instead of whalebone we have the workout. The ideal shape is achieved through diet and exercise. And for those who fall short, there are Spanx. *Plus ça change!*

Ooh! la! la!

'Gaiety Girl' — the fabulous new Gossard girdle promises to make the best of every fashion-conscious customer you have! Now it's up to *YOU!*

The girdle that has everything the young woman looks for in underfashion . . .

- **waist cinching**
- **tummy and hip controlling**
- **lightly boned *permanent* shape**
- **fits low over the seat**
- **fashion-following lines**

S. 23-24
M. 25-27
L. 28-30

39/9 *Retail*

ORDER NOW.   STOCKS ARE READY FOR YOU

YOUR SELLING MADE EASY WITH NATION-WIDE ADVERTISING

SILK SKIN

GOSSARD LTD.,
Gossard House, Heddon St,
Regent St, London, W.1

Gossard

Gossard   gives you the most consistent advertising coverage in the trade

MARIA CALLAS
The diva who reinvented herself

She was a prima donna assoluta in the time-honoured tradition. Her unique voice, musicianship, magnetic stage presence and flaming temperament ensured she was in the news wherever she went. Her playground was the ranks of the highest international society. She dated billionaires. On and off the stage, she was glamour incarnate.

Born in New York in 1923, she first became an opera star at La Scala in Milan in the early 1950s. By the time she was ready for her American debut at the Metropolitan Opera, she had crafted herself into the image of a global superstar. She had shed 70 pounds and weighed in at a slim 135. At 5 feet 8 inches tall, and with a face made striking by her broad cheekbones, she was one of the handsomest women of the operatic stage. Her reputation was such that announcements of her appearances generated long lines outside the box office of the opera houses where she was to sing. Yves Saint Laurent and Christian Dior designed for her.

To her audiences she became a figure of almost mythical stature. The last time she sang in Carnegie Hall, a voice bellowed from the balcony: 'You are opera!' Her fans were resolutely loyal even as she was beset by vocal difficulties at the end of her career. To them she was the one singer who represented opera as theatre – the artist who lived her roles and made them come to life. Her recordings make her one of the bestselling opera stars to this day.

The Austrian American composer Arnold Schoenberg later said of her, 'Tall, slim, commanding, exotically beautiful, Miss Callas had a unique combination of electricity and brains.'

With her weight loss and image change, Maria Callas became one of the most beautiful singers ever. No longer simply an opera star, she became La Divina. Her popularity had increased dramatically. People idolized her, and in the 1950s Maria Callas became an international celebrity.

MARTHA GRAHAM
Dancer of the century

In the 1950s, Martha Graham (1894–1991) raised modern dance to a new level of popularity, helping to forge a new language of movement. She remains a towering figure to this day. In 1951 she was among the people who established the dance programme at the Juilliard School in New York City.

Among her students were Bette Davis, Liza Minnelli and film director Woody Allen. Madonna, also a pupil, tells the story in an interview for BBC radio of her first encounter with one of the few people who ever intimidated her: 'She was part Norma Desmond in Sunset Boulevard. The rest of her was a cross between a Kabuki dancer and a nun. She just looked at me with what I thought was interest but was probably only disapproval. She was both small and big at the same time. It was my first encounter with a goddess.'

In 1998, *Time* magazine named her as the 'Dancer of the Century' and as one of the most important people of the twentieth century. Graham's creativity crossed artistic boundaries and embraced every artistic genre. She collaborated with and commissioned work from the leading visual artists, musicians and designers of her day, including the sculptor Isamu Noguchi and the fashion designers Halston, Donna Karan and Calvin Klein. She used costume as a pivotal device in the creation of visual effect on stage. Designer Rifat Ozbek dedicated a collection to her in 1989, and as recently as 2011 Marni founder and designer Consuelo Castiglioni cited her as one of her key inspirations.

Costumes were a vital part of Martha Graham's dance pieces. The swirling jerseys were integral to the overall visual effect. In her everyday wardrobe she favoured pieces that enhanced the movement of her body, even if she was simply walking down the street.

NORMAN PARKINSON
Gentleman photographer

Norman Parkinson (1913–90) started his career in the stuffy world of 1930s society portraiture. 'All the girls had their knees bolted together,' he remembered. As a fashion photographer, he much preferred to take models out of the studio and into the real world. The style he developed owes much to his double life as photographer and farmer. His love of the country, he said, was 'part of the secret of why I think and see as I do'.

Before Parkinson's arrival at British *Vogue* in the early 1940s, the magazine, then only starting to explore colour photography, had relied on imported photographers from Europe and America, and on material borrowed from its American sister publication. Once editorial budgets were restored after the war, Parkinson's English pastoralism gave British *Vogue* a distinct identity. Parkinson pioneered fashion shoots in exotic locations at a time when long-haul travel was still in its infancy. Foreign assignments in the 1950s took him to India, Australia, Jamaica, Tobago and Haiti.

Parkinson became a huge hit in America, not least because of his distinctive demeanour, which established him as a personality quite as much as his models and sitters. He became a walking six-foot-five caricature of a dandyish Englishman with officer-class mustachios and furled umbrella.

He was rigorous in concealing the hard work that accompanied every assignment, but his painstaking preparation before every picture was taken is remembered by those who worked with him. He made light of the graft, preferring to maintain the appearance of a spontaneous style. In later years, he conceded that 'almost every photograph that is particularly appealing and true has been arranged and rehearsed'.

In the 1980s, Parkinson said he wished his obituary to read simply: 'He took photography out of the embalming trade.'

Norman Parkinson much preferred to work out of doors. He said, 'A studio is like an operating theatre. You go there to get part of yourself removed.' He took his models into the countryside, introducing a degree of realism. But the relaxed approach belied a rigorous perfectionism which made him a lovable taskmaster.

STILETTOES

Roger Vivier's greatest legacy

Both men and women had laboured through the war years in unflattering boots and shoes. Comfort and practicality had been the sole priorities. As a result, the postwar world was in desperate need of footwear fashion.

Heels had been getting progressively higher as hemlines became shorter throughout the twentieth century. High heels became the ne plus ultra, particularly in Hollywood, where actresses wore slim sparkly heels that made the more traditional, mid-height French heel look positively dowdy by comparison.

With the launch of Dior's New Look, it behoved shoe designers to step up to the mark with something equally ground-breaking. Enter French shoe designer Roger Vivier (1907–98), who mastered the technology that enabled women to wear a teetering heel that would perfectly set off a Christian Dior dress. It was strong stuff, and it was an instant hit. Ladies were offered lessons to help them walk properly, and there was considerable alarm over the damage stilettos might do to polished floors.

The 1950s stiletto was more innovation than invention, since women had been known to wear a version of what we now refer to as a stiletto as far back as Victorian times. But the steel-strengthened, pencil-thin heel was Vivier's great contribution. If the Frenchman perfected the engineering, it was the Italian Salvatore Ferragamo who gave the shoe its name, however, coining the term 'stiletto' from the Greek word *stylos*, meaning 'pillar'.

Roger Vivier had no truck with democracy. His shoes were unashamedly luxurious. He designed for several couturiers, including Schiaparelli in the 1930s, but notably for Christian Dior, with whom he redefined fashion in the 1950s and early 60s. He was the only one of Dior's collaborators permitted to have a credit on the final design: 'Christian Dior cré par Roger Vivier' was marked inside every shoe.

'BABE' PALEY
Style perfectionist

Truman Capote called 'Babe' Paley, C Z Guest and Gloria Guinness his 'swans'. From her marriage to CBS founder Bill Paley in 1947, Barbara Cushing Mortimer Paley (1915–78) reigned as high priestess of fashion and the social arts until her death in 1978.

Blessed with a slender figure and distinctively pale skin, she honed her style as a fashion editor at US *Vogue*, where she also modelled. As a divorced single mother living on a meagre budget with two young children, she was nonetheless able to maintain an enviable wardrobe. Charles James, Chanel, Hubert de Givenchy and Norman Norell were among those who gave her clothes, realizing that hers was a very valuable stamp of approval.

She later married the fabulously wealthy Bill Paley, made the Best Dressed List 14 times and became an inspiration for store mannequins, fashion illustrators and photographers alike. A painstaking perfectionist, she washed and ironed her custom-made heavy white piqué blouses herself, 'because she wouldn't ask anyone else to do it'.

At a time when society women favoured sets of matching jewels, it was typical of her style to mix her precious Verdura and Schlumberger jewellery with cheap costume pieces. When, in her fifties, she decided to let her hair go grey, masses of women followed suit. Trouser suits might have been a controversial choice for a smart luncheon, but when she wore them they became the height of modern chic. When photographers snapped her with a scarf casually tied to the side of her handbag (she had removed it en route because it was too warm), it became a fashion 'look'.

Babe Paley was a 'stylist' before the term was coined, making clothes uniquely her own. Ropes of pearls might be twined about the wrist or 'thrown to the back', as her friend Oscar de la Renta recalled in *Vogue* in 2009. 'Whatever she wore,' the designer said, 'she wore in a way you would never forget.'

Another of Truman Capote's 'swans', is shown here being photographed by her husband William Paley beside the pool of their cottage in Round Hill, Jamaica. Eleanor Lambert, founder of the Best Dressed List, dubbed her 'The Super Dresser of all Time'.

BARBIE

All a 50s woman could want to be

Back in the early 1950s there was a little girl called Barbara ('Barbie') Handler, whose mother Ruth reckoned it was important for young girls to imagine life as an adult through the world of play, and therefore made her a doll on which to project her fantasies of grown-up life. It was convenient that Ruth and her husband Elliot had, some years earlier, founded the Mattel Corporation in their garage. Nonetheless, advertising executives at first rejected the idea, considering it both too expensive to develop and of limited appeal.

Ruth Handler persisted, however, and in February 1959 Barbie Millicent Roberts arrived, measuring 11½ inches tall. She debuted at the American Toy Fair in New York City. For her first outing she was a blonde in a bold black-and-white striped swimsuit, with open-toed shoes, sunglasses and earrings. New, suburban lifestyles revolved around the consumption of luxury goods, and Barbie had lots of them – the raciest cars, the coolest outfits and the most wanted accessories.

She was an instant hit, and in the first year 351,000 dolls were sold at three dollars each. Barbie's appearance was a precise reflection of Western society's attitude to women at the time. With her long legs, small waist and voluptuous, pert bosom, she was considered the ideal. She had a freckle-free complexion with long lashes and just a hint of makeup.

The box she arrived in was covered in stylized fashion drawings. Her wardrobe's key looks were a fluffy nightwear ensemble (perfect for sleepovers), an outfit for hosting a weekend 'barbie-Q', and of course a wedding dress. Barbie represented all that the marketing fraternity believed a woman could want to be in the 1950s – glamorous, famous, wealthy and popular.

A testament to Barbie's evergreen fashion status came with the celebration of her fiftieth anniversary, when a runway show in her honour formed part of the New York Collections. Fifty household-name American designers took part, including Diane von Furstenberg, Calvin Klein and Vera Wang.

LORD SNOWDON

Capturing the vibrancy of a new age

In the 1950s, London was exciting international interest with its burgeoning music and fashion youth cultures. One of the pioneers of the spirited new English style was Antony Armstrong-Jones (1930–), later Earl of Snowdon. After studying architecture at Cambridge, he started his career as a portrait photographer. But by 1956 he was working on advertising and fashion shoots for *Tatler*, *Vogue*, *Harper's Bazaar* and the *Daily Express* newspaper.

The young Armstrong-Jones captured all the excitement of London's cultural renaissance and the unique energy that was driving its fledgling fashion industry. On the one hand, there was the cult of the 'angry young men', such as the writers John Osborne and Kingsley Amis, mouthpieces for a generation disillusioned with traditional English society. On the other, there was the amazing success of Mary Quant and the boutique called Bazaar which she opened on the King's Road in 1955.

Until then, fashion had been limited to the environs of the salons whose hallowed portals were open by appointment only. London's young fashion fans and its emerging designers were of a similar age and had similar tastes and interests. Quant, much like Coco Chanel and Claire McCardell, was a designer who was not only a fashion designer in the way she dressed, but was also one of the most influential trend-setters; in her hands, fashion was low-priced, ready to wear and immediately available.

Snowdon captured that atmosphere. His photographs are memorable for their wit and zest and immediacy, and his young models look like they are having a fabulous time in odd situations. It might not have been photorealism, but it did define the glamour and vibrancy of a new age.

Snowdon's fashion pictures were spontaneous moments caught on camera when no one else was looking. A woman marches across the street (right), another totters about to fall into a river, and a third knocks over glasses as she jumps up to embrace a man. His models carried on life regardless of the lens that observed them.

GLORIA GUINNESS

The magnificent minimalist

With her famous 'Nefertiti profile' and uncluttered approach to fashion, Gloria Guinness (1912–80), along with her fellow 'swans', ruled the style world from the 1950s until her death in 1980. A Mexican of humble origins, she married the English banking magnate Loel Guinness, and at a stroke wiped out the less than impeccable shadow cast by two previous marriages and a mysterious war record.

Guinness wrote her own script. 'When she was poor she told everyone that fur coats were tacky,' remembered the Venezuelan TV host Reinaldo Herrera. And about the only thing unfashionable about her, in a set where modesty was prized, were the sometimes crass declarations she made: 'Chic? It is absolutely innate. I was born with it.' And as she told W magazine in 1976, 'I've never worn costume jewellery in my life. It's really self-defeating. Why should a man buy a woman real jewellery when she wears false pieces?'

In Paris before the war John Fairchild noted: 'La Guinness was the chicest of all in a black cardigan and black skirt.' As she climbed the social ladder, she had money for more extravagant clothes but never lost her minimalist look. Wealth only allowed her to carry her art of under-dressing to a new level. Cristóbal Balenciaga was her favourite designer. He said she was the most elegant woman he dressed. 'I don't follow fashion,' she told an interviewer coolly, 'I believe in consistency. Every time I have changed my look I have been unhappy.'

Guinness accessorized couture dresses with cheap scarves, and when asked what she wore at home she said, 'comfortable robes I pick up for $12.95 a piece in Manhattan'. 1950s formality did not stop her making a look out of a Moroccan djellaba or accessorizing simple pants with a South American poncho. More recently, 'Glorious Guinness' was the muse for Michael Kors' resort show.

She told Balenciaga where to place the buttons and backed Castillo when he left Lanvin to open his own couture house. But while she had access to the best, she could also, as Oscar de la Renta once said, 'make an ordinary Hanes T-shirt look chic,' and would famously accessorize a couture dress with a scarf from Kmart.

HITCHCOCK'S 'FROSTY BLONDES'
Highly stylized sex appeal

The director Alfred Hitchcock fetishized the 'frosty blonde', and over the course of his career honed his image of the perfect woman. A succession of beautiful actresses combined feminine refinement and sex appeal in a way that was meticulously stylized. Hitchcock heroines tended to be lovely, cool blondes who seemed proper at first, but when aroused by passion or danger responded in a sensual, animal or even criminal way.

While they all shared some qualities, it would be a mistake to view them as cookie-cutter blondes. The continuous and symbolic evolution of the Hitchcock heroine made them very different from each other.

Greta Garbo, in *Stage Fright* (1950), was one of the earliest of the type and a knowing, glacial heroine. Kim Novak was more voluptuous, and throughout *Vertigo* (1958) tantalizingly wore her hair in a tightly coiled French twist – a thinly veiled Hitchcockian metaphor, of course, for tightly coiled feminine passion. Eva Marie Saint in *North by Northwest* (1959) possessed, by comparison, a brittle and seductive perfection.

Even the choice of lipstick colour could be loaded with symbolism. Hitchcock's 'good' female characters wore cool, barely-there make-up to minimize their sexuality, while red lipstick blatantly signified sex. For instance, Kim Novak as the idealized Madeleine in *Vertigo* has light-pink lips and blonde hair, but as 'imperfect' Judy has red hair and red lips.

But it was Grace Kelly who was the quintessential 'snow-covered volcano'. Kelly was one of the definitive beauties of the 1950s. An icon of elegance and refinement, she effortlessly portrayed the haughty allure that so appealed to Hitchcock, for whom she starred in *Dial M for Murder* (1954), *Rear Window* (1954) and *To Catch a Thief* (1955). 'You know why I favour sophisticated blondes in my films?' the director once asked. 'We're after the drawing-room type, the real ladies, who become whores once they're in the bedroom.'

Cary Grant and Eva Marie Saint in *North by Northwest,* (1959). Hitchcock's icy heroines have it all: beauty, brains, and bravery. They don't shy away from the heat of the action when the bullets start flying. Often they're the ones risking their lives to save the men. And through it all, they manage to stay perfectly coiffed and radiant.

It is probably no coincidence that, with thousands of demobbed men on the job market, the ideology of the feminine mystique influenced many women in the 1950s to leave the workforce and return home to play the roles of wife and mother. Those women who did continue to work were expected to conform to a rigid image of appropriate womanly behaviour and appearance.

In 1959 Edith Head (see page 56), the legendary costume designer in Hollywood and one of the most successful career women of the decade, defined the style dilemma working women faced: 'No man wants a brisk executive at the dinner table and no man wants a too alluring creature gliding around his office.' The 1959 movie *The Best of Everything* was an early forerunner of *Sex and the City*, a cautionary tale about life in the big city for three young women seeking their independence at that time.

Like many of the working women of the 1950s, Caroline Bender, the central figure, takes a job in order to become more financially independent, but considers it as really just a way to pass the time while she waits to get married. Back then, the spectre of spinsterhood – a status that could be achieved even before one had turned 25 – loomed large.

Caroline wails, 'What is it about women like us that makes you hold us so cheaply? Aren't we the special ones from the best homes and the best colleges? I know the world outside isn't full of rainbows and happy endings, but to you, aren't we even decent?' By the end of the movie she is a hat-wearing executive. Female executives in those days wore their hats all day long. Having a hat on gave the impression that they were always preparing to go out, that they had somewhere important to be.

The Best of Everything (1959), starred Hope Lange, Diane Baker, Joan Crawford and former model Suzy Parker (see page 84). 'Any time we girls have to go to work, the result, historically, is that we do things better. I mean, gentlemen will go to the trouble of keeping office hours, holding board meetings, and getting Mr Gallup to make a poll in order to reach a decision any blonde could reach while refurbishing her lipstick.' Anita Loos.

INDEX

PICTURE CREDITS

FURTHER READING

Ballard, Bettina (1960), *In My Fashion*, David Mckay Co

Charles-Roux, Edmonde (2010), *Chanel and Her World*, Vendome Press

Clarke Keogh, Pamela and De Givenchy, Hubert (2009), *Audrey Style*, Aurum Press Ltd

De Beauvoir, Simone (1976), *Brigitte Bardot and the Lolita Syndrome*, Arno Press

Devlin, Polly (1979), *Vogue Book of Fashion Photography*, Simon & Schuster

Edkins, Diana and Tapert, Annette (2005), *The Power of Style*, Crown Publications

Ferrucio, Frank (2007), *Diamond to Dust: The Life and Death of Jayne Mansfield*, Outskirts Press

Hansford, Andrew (2011), *Dressing Marilyn*, Goodman Books

Johnson, Joyce (2006), *Minor Characters: A Beat Memoir*, Methuen Publishing Ltd

Jones, Dylan (1990), *Haircults*, Thames & Hudson Ltd

Jorgensen, Jay (2010), *Edith Head*, Running Press

Jouve, Marie-Andree and Dermonex, Jacqueline (2004), *Balenciaga*, Assouline

Leret, Vincent and Nissen, Sylvie (2010), *René Gruau's First Century*, Thalia Publishing

Liaut, Jean-Noel (2000), *Hubert de Givenchy*, Grasset

Loos, Anita (1974), *Kiss Hollywood Goodbye*, W.H. Allen / Virgin Books

Marsh, Graham and Trynka, Paul (2005), *Denim*, Aurum Press Ltd

McDowell, Colin (1994), *Shoes*, Thames & Hudson Ltd

Mulvagh, Jane (1988), *Vogue History of 20th Century Fashion*, Viking

Rennolds Millbank, Caroline (1989), *New York Fashion: The Evolution of American Style*, Harry N. Abrams, Inc.

Taraborelli, J. Randy (2003), *Once Upon a Time*, Sidgwick & Jackson Ltd

Veillon, Dominique (1990), *La Mode sous l'Occupation*, Payot

Vreeland, Diana (2010), *Allure*, Chronicle Books

Yohannan, Kohle and Nolf, Nancy (1999), *Clare McCardell: Redefining Modernism*, Harry N. Abrams, Inc.

CREDITS

First published in 2012 by Conran Octopus Ltd a part of Octopus Publishing Group, Endeavour House, 189 Shaftesbury Avenue, London WC2H 8JY www.octopusbooks.co.uk

An Hachette UK Company www.hachette.co.uk

Distributed in the US by Hachette Book Group USA, 237 Park Avenue, New York, NY 10017 USA

Distributed in Canada by Canadian Manda Group, 165 Dufferin Street, Toronto, Ontario, Canada M6K 3H6

British Library Cataloguing-in-Publication Data. A catalogue record for this book is available from the British Library.

Text written by: Paula Reed

Publisher: Alison Starling
Consultant Editor: Deyan Sudjic
Senior Editor: Sybella Stephens
Editor: Robert Anderson
Art Director: Jonathan Christie
Design: Untitled
Picture Research: Anne-Marie Hoines & Sara Rumens
Production: Lucy Carter

ISBN: 978 1 84091 603 4
Printed in China